EAST COAST
Heartbreak

AMY LAESSLE-MORGAN

EAST COAST HEARTBREAK

Copyright © 2024 by Amy Laessle-Morgan. All rights reserved.
Printed in the United States of America. No part of this book may be used or reproduced in any manner whatsoever without the author's prior written permission, except for review uses permitted by copyright law.

ISBN: 979-8-218-50557-8 (Paperback)

Library of Congress Control Number: 2024921975

Presented by:
Neon Sparrow Press ©
FIRST EDITION

@ultramarine_poetry

Amy Laessle-Morgan

Preface

The first time I stood on the edge of the Cape, it felt like I had come to the end of the world. The wind carried with it the scent of salty sea, and all I could see was endless water ahead of me, the waves breaking with a kind of reckless, chaotic beauty. In that moment, I understood something about myself: sometimes the storm must crash over you before calm arrives. I was there to escape the heaviness, trying to find solace in beauty, but the truth was, I wasn't just looking for peace; I was looking for a way back to myself, to the person I had been before life felt unrecognizable.

As I stood there, I couldn't help but think of one of my favorite literary works, *The Great Gatsby*. Every time I find myself in a new place, I seek out a used bookstore, hoping to discover a different edition to add to my collection. There's a certain magic in weathered pages, a reminder of something tangible you can hold. I like to think of all the people's hands this book has also passed through, having been touched by F. Scott Fitzgerald's words. I've always been captivated by the story of a man who clings to an idealized love from his past, striving to recreate a dream that eludes him. His pursuits resonate deeply with my own experiences of loss and longing. In the same way Gatsby reaches for a distant green light, I find myself reaching back toward a version of myself I can no longer return to, trying to reconcile the past with the present.

East Coast Heartbreak is more than just an anthology of poems. It's a map of my life born of those storms. It's about the grief of losing someone suddenly, the longing for things that slipped through my hands, and the way something as simple as the ocean's pull always seems to bring me back to the peace I need. It's about who I was and who I'm becoming, ever tied to the places and people that shaped me while also carving out my own identity for what seems like the first time.

The book is divided into six sections, each representing a different phase of this journey. Whether you read this collection from front to back or dive into pieces that speak to you at random, thank you for being here as we are all just trying to navigate the messiness and chaos that is life.

"So we beat on, boats against the current, borne back ceaselessly into the past."
— **F. Scott Fitzgerald, The Great Gatsby**

Contents

Nostalgia 11
Nostalgia 12
Lazy Sunbathers 13
Anarchy In Bloom 14
Of Gods and Dive Bars 15

Wander 19
Wander 20
Dance Lessons 22
An Evening In Fall River 23
The Fall 24
Driftwood Beach 25
High Tide 26
Cape Cod June 27
Savannah 29
East Coast Heartbreak 30
Along Marginal Way 31
Racepoint Beach 32
Midnight in Salem 33
Karma For Graceland 35

If We Make it Through the Night 39
In Time 40
Capture the Lightning 41
January 10th 42
Forgotten the Surface 43
Anchored 44
Sometime in the Mourning 45
Broken 46
I Am Not 48
Eve After The Fall 49
Writing a Poem to a Brick Wall at 4 a.m. on a Thursday 50

Chasing Echoes ... 52
If We Make It Through the Night ... 53
Swallow ... 54
Beyond the Green Grass ... 55

Alive ... 57

Tourist ... 58
Downpour ... 59
Patient ... 60
September's Breath of Poetry ... 61
The Lion and the Moon ... 62
Alive ... 63
Mixtape ... 64
Anthem ... 65
Startled Air ... 66
Labyrinths ... 67
Bibliophile ... 68
Seamless ... 69
Respire ... 70
Maps ... 71
Smolder ... 72
Bliss ... 73

Ashes to Ashes ... 75

Between Insomnia and Fading Lights ... 76
Fade ... 78
The Movie's Ending ... 79
Oh, So Tired ... 82
The Sweet and the Stung ... 83
Under the Overpass ... 84
Grey Area ... 86
Time Bomb Girl ... 88
Ashes to Ashes ... 89
Cipher ... 90

Gilded Oblivion ... 91
The Taste of Arsenic ... 92
The Fading Asters ... 93
Afterthought ... 95

The Season of Holding On ... 99

Lost Dreamer ... 100
The Marble Faun ... 102
The Stray ... 104
The Season of Holding On ... 106
Unapologetic ... 107
Acknowledgments ... 111
About The Author ... 113

Nostalgia

*– I held my ear to your chest
and heard echoes
of my past self*

Nostalgia

Nostalgia casts her sepia tone over the past
she is that sweet ache that comes from remembering
in various unrevealed layers
yet to be peeled back

We were oblivious to our golden hour
only recognizing its shiny value
as it slipped from our palms
into the ether

Monochrome nights passed away too quickly,
and technicolor daybreak met us too soon
between barbed wire phantom barriers
we failed to realize
we were living

Connecting hastened pauses
and slow, steady breaths
raw and unfiltered
we met within moments and the silence between them
never needing to find the right words

I held my ear to your chest
and heard echoes of my past self
intoxicating and still
yet so hard to leave

The good times flood our minds
good times that were just time
and the moments were everything
even when we didn't know
all that we were doing
was simply being alive

Lazy Sunbathers

We plunged into pools of boundless aquamarine adventure
embraced by the infinite warmth of a molten-gold sun

Carefree, chlorine-filled days flood my memory
the water's expanse shimmering of turquoise, beckoning us with promises
of what seemed like vast oceans to wide, wonder-filled eyes

The lazy sunbathers of our generation
basked in the honeyed glow of endless summer days
our laughter mingling gently with cicada hums

In my mind, we are forever
chasing dreams with butterfly nets
woven from endless enthusiasm

Anarchy In Bloom

July humidity melts and peels back lush leaves of gladiolus blooms
a flower born of contradictions, elegant yet audacious
sword-like leaves unsheathed, promising both danger and splendor
the rebel of the garden
flipping off convention with every blaze of petal

We dig and plant them in holes deep and defiant
co-conspirators in midnight plots casting shadows
like elongated question marks bursting through
with revelations in tender light,
they sway red, pink, yellow—each hue but a promise
etched in petals, then broken
like brittle love, so fragile and fleeting amongst summer heat
remain silent, biding time plotting revolutions
yet bend beneath the weight of mortality

Every kiss stolen by the breeze
while whispered secrets lost and faded
wave silent goodbyes under the setting sun

Something—once vibrant, now ember they thrived
as we beg to emerge as a beacon of defiance in a sea of conformity
a refusal to accept mediocrity

Of Gods and Dive Bars

They say the gods envy mortality
I wonder how true this is
as we're knee-deep in a smoky haze of this forgotten dive
air thick with secrets and the scent of old leather
neon flickering above our heads like dying stars

Your eyes hold so many stories
that liquid fire coaxes from your lips
these aren't your garden-variety bedtime stories
they spill and shatter like glass across the room
you warn me too much time here
turns poets into prophets and prophets into fools

We seek out truth
and taste forbidden fruit
that, like forgotten sins, sometimes burns
as walls weep poetry
of fire and despair

You tell me the gods are just cosmic drunks
who sip the Milky Way,
chasing comets like lost lovers,
but mortals, they're the real poets

You joke I remind you of the archetypal maiden Persephone,
who doesn't know yet who she is,
what strengths she possesses or what she truly desires

Outside, we twirl, arms outstretched towards heaven as
I scribble feverishly everything into my notebook that you had spoken
words like the first blooms of spring,
burst to life with colors I wish to press between pages of my heart
and preserve their essence
because tonight and every night
you've always been the verse I can't shake

You lean in close
so I can feel the warmth of your breath on my skin and whisper,
"Your brief, beautiful blaze of existence
lasts but a second,
so write damn it,
until your veins bleed ink
and your tears birth constellations,
never stop chasing the chaos
and I promise always to leave you
with a head full of stars and a heart aflame"

Wander

*— It was such a pleasure
to burn so radiant
beside you*

Wander

This must be the place
between silence and whispers
where shooting stars
birth moments of light in the heavens
these fleeting, fading flashes of existence
from the confines of a black-and-white realm
beyond notions
the vast expanse where our souls coalesce
serene under a boundless sky

Where love and understanding softly align
forming safe spaces, and all prejudice fades away
compassion takes root like wild thyme under our feet,
ego holds no sway

This must be the place
I tread barefoot upon lush paths of clover
stumbling many times, crossed with introspection
beneath me but also far away
ushering in this moment
where groups change swiftly
and swells of laughter become easier to produce
minute by minute

New arrivals, wanderers, soul-crossed stragglers
who weave here and glide through the sea-change of color
the constantly changing light
accept this celebration
the party has just begun

This must be the place
where water bathes bare-skinned dreams
underneath a twilight orchestra conducted by moonglow
as this orb of night pulls the tides
and you and I closer together
amidst sweet wisteria-laden air
like a gently plotted-out constellation
a universe stitched together in stardust patches, consuming
it was such a pleasure to burn so radiant beside you

Dance Lessons

A soul on the edge of its own disappearance
I felt the warmth of your hand guiding me
over polished amber floor
a first of many lessons to learn

I did not ask for these songs of sorrow
they find their way to unwelcome ears all the same
resonating through crimson pillars of a bruised, acrimonious heart

As we drift through dimly lit doorways of memory
my spirit finds delicate solace in the glow of your minty-green
gaze, spinning through time's intricate patterns

A dance of smiles veils discontent,
creating the rhythm
of life's fleeting story

An Evening In Fall River

Empty streets fill with fragrant petrichor
as raindrops begin to fall, kissing arid pavement
the world seems to sigh with pleasure, as do I
we unconsciously inhale deeply
to savor great lung-fulls of downpour's seductive scent

Hand in hand, we find ourselves
alongside the humid New England evening
as rows of streetlamps punctuate gossamer orbs
and cast their glow against vast, boundless sky

The weathered soles of our shoes carry us
past the corner of Second and Borden
against hydrangea-flecked lawns and timeworn houses
down alleyways, annexed by thunder and ghosts

Vetiver incense of damp earth
curls through stoic buildings erupted from the ashes,
rebuilt like my faith – because of you

In this moment, within the clasp of your hand
amongst looming night specters
all my haunted notions of hurting
set themselves free

The Fall

The blue August evening has soaked itself into the sky
and tumbled down gently amongst the trees
flooding cracks between pavement
where weeds and wildflowers grow as harsh and fast
as my love for you
untamed, unmanaged

These warm, tender nights drift away anymore
as I reflect on how perfectly my cheek finds its home
within the depression of your shoulder

so easily loved
so hard to love

Within these nights of easeful conspiracy
when we still believed in vibrant dreams of summer
the trees agreed it was all for the best
beneath new moon shimmers
casting silver-lapis silhouettes of retrospect

Now, all we have is this elusive past
that forever remains
a harmonious misconception of memory

Nothing spells fall quite like love
and nothing dims the light in your eyes
that flickered far enough away
to be interpreted as we liked

For it is always the loose ends that hang us

Driftwood Beach

palm leaves part ways
we escape oppressive humidity
into another world
ripe with mystery

a landscape of gnarled and twisted trees lie stricken by erosion,
shrines of ancient driftwood line sun-kissed saltwater shores
their firm grasps on the past uprooted,
crooked beams above crashing opalescent blue waves

our bare feet climb these slippery, wet vessels of time
drawing us in closer,
as we dance in the eventide of our finest hour
teasing horizons between darkness and light

seagulls scream warnings
as the ocean pulls back the seafoam hem of her gossamer garment
revealing delicate seashell-laden beaches beneath us
rust-tinged horseshoe crabs play a fiddling melody

outstretched arms greet enchanted heavens
we ascend sun-bleached thrones of pine
surveying the beauty within this graveyard of trees
adorned with rose-colored sunbeams
paying homage to life's counterpart

everything grand must end
but somehow, your cleverness escaped this fate
preserved with a salty-aired kiss,
resting eternal,
bedded down upon sands of time

High Tide

Standing on sandy shores, the ocean breathes salty
crashing waves envelop bare feet
warm sun caressing skin elicits familiar sensations
of thoughts when I recall your good-natured smile
nature lends her beauty, healing wounds, and lifting spirits

Lying down before the tide that is nearing,
an unexpected baptism from darkness to light
to wash away numbness
crystal clear resolutions slip like sand through spread fingers

If only I could walk again through this moment
leaving water-flooded footprints
clutching foresight and hindsight
equipped with knowledge and answers of which path to stroll down

Still never forgetting the moonlight and softness,
how it all came together

The pull of the ocean
lives forever in my soul

Cape Cod June

Spring had broken me
as June sweltered out with her last hot week
fanning raging fires
where the strangle of smoke
convened with the aching inside my heart
radiant and brilliant
leaving a husk of regret
that soon followed all things I've ever loved

I've especially learned to miss
the blushing moon among star-speckled skies
of those warm New England evenings
among lush greenery and sugar-sand beaches
coated thick with sea salt air

This ocean connects me to you
her ripple waves rushing in
like fingers strumming a familiar song
as raspberry sorbet and cotton candy clouds dissolve
into tints of love and desire

When I think of all the kisses that have melted away in my mouth
and fading things we will only know
but we will have forgotten soon,
all we could see and none we could share
maybe I've dreamt them all

I want to swim out,
stir the surface of the sea
give old ghosts a way to roam

Take me out to her
somewhere beautiful and powerful
drifting deep beneath her satin foam
as wisdom and years pass away
salty tears masked
so you shall not know
this heaviness I feel

Savannah

I walk in shadows of history
rows of houses burst with color
I am amorous of antebellum architecture
a love poem written in cobblestone

surrounded by fountains and old fortunes
branches bearded with Spanish moss hang down
dripping sweet southern charm
like Tupelo honey

a bridal veil of magnolias
scents the warm breeze
and marries my heart forever
to this seductive city

East Coast Heartbreak

I once saw true love
alongside the highway
at a gas station
in Albany, NY
framed through the back window
of the car ahead

He casually tousled her hair,
their eyes and foreheads a whisper apart,
her laughter the only sound piercing through
the staleness of gas station air

And as I stood there
emotionally bankrupt, running on empty
feeling a deep ache
I wondered if maybe someone
should cut me open,
like one of those Operation games
and see if I'm missing
all the butterflies in the stomach

As they drove off onto
I-90 E, to write their own vows
on the back of a fast-food napkin,
I couldn't shake the thought
if only I had a match handy
because what's a little existential dread
without the threat of combustion
amidst clichés and carbon monoxide
as we drive off into that East Coast heartbreak

Along Marginal Way

I watched the setting sun mirror my sinking heart
over Perkins Bay in this quaint harbor town of Ogunquit, Maine
painting heaven with strokes of despair
flaunting purples and pink-faded blush that quickly
surrender to ocean deep blues
within a shroud of jagged rock edges, tumbled smooth by salty indigo sea

I made a wish this briny air and untamed wild could hold me steady,
while I nursed this heartache like a hobby
bleeding out on these rocks crimson for such casual cruelty
a feral beast of beauty,
the thrill isn't in the flowers' crown
but in the reckless abandon of the climb to pick them
you loved to watch me dance in Sisyphean loops on slippery ledges
for daisies you never watered or wanted

Schooled in the masochistic economics of buy-one-get-one-free
heartbreak with the price of inflation
to learn in the end, you can't count on much these days but ocean tides
they always come back and recede like a well-timed tragedy
their waves of mutilation
crashing through lies and apathy
to wash away the bleeding
and bathe you in the embrace of nature's unjudging light
in the wild heart of Maine, where the cliffs still dare to kiss the sky

Racepoint Beach

The heat of a New England summer is a madness all its own
a fever dream where the only relief is
a faint solution of ocean spray
carried to shore by a sympathetic breeze
it kisses my lips

I'm starved for the salty taste of your skin
forged in the furnace
of molten sun that hangs above us heavy like a verdict,
so ripe it bleeds citrus orange light across the horizon

Sand clings to me with a hunger that echoes your touch
it's a cruel sweetness
these grains of sand hold fast to skin, showing no mercy
untethered by tan lines
within softness and sorrow, I feel liberation

We could lie down, let the world spin on without us,
but the sands of time are a miser that cannot be bought or sold
they instead, must be spent until we are bankrupt of them all
for some things are too vast to hold,
they can't be bottled like love
and that tango of skin on the Cape beach

Watch me burn, becoming smoke on the wind
and if you remember anything,
let it be the heat,
the all-consuming fire of what we were

Midnight in Salem

We coasted into Salem against the onyx-velvet witching hour
perhaps for spells or spirits,
you know I need to exorcise
these ghosts trapped inside me

As I bought up every skeleton key candle
and incense stick in the little Apothecary
you laughed at the notion
that a pinch of Salem's finest could thread back together
edges of a patchwork heart, frayed by failures

A series of scars and stitches
I keep tearing out, prolonging healing
hoping some inner crucible alchemy
will relieve the itch
turning pain into jewelry

I'm still trying to wring the dusk-tide from my pupils
in this town of Hawthorne and Monopoly
as we walked through its square
past the bars
where poets drown in art and sorrows

Cobblestone streets
trip me up along the way
but I hold steady to your strong arm
and beautiful sincerity
in the midst of all these black cats
and poetry of haunted pasts
maybe there is still some glittering-gold magic left inside me

I'm bewitched by your selflessness and smile
I could die right now, but I want this to last a moment longer
because life is too short
and I want to live for you

You held my hand through cemetery gates
as we read silent sentinels and epitaphs
of etched reminders that time is only borrowed
and may all end tomorrow

Not today, you assure me,
while our love still pulsates and breathes
but when the end comes
may it find us in each other's arms
bedded down between knotty oak trees

Karma For Graceland

Summer of '92, a red-hot blistering haze of heat and teenage
rebellion a spiteful heart full of New Wave & Grunge pulsed through
my veins as sunburnt legs stuck to slick, pleather, sweat-soaked car
seats
my father's Elvis cassette drones on a relentless loop
as if Elvis himself had composed this death march to monotony
as we entered the gilded gateway to my own personal hell
of sequined jumpsuits and sideburns: Graceland

Rolled eyes and audible sighs echoed within thick verdant
plastic foliage of jungle room kitsch
ironically, feeling "so lonely I could die," I sat,
contemplating my existence
in front of reflection pools whose clarity gave new meanings of,
"I'm caught in a trap, I can't walk out"

Funny thing, fate, its cosmic punchline delivered decades later,
on a blustery Cape beach
I glimpse my son—a reluctant traveler of new age
digital screen haze—in a town of lobsters and Kennedys,
scowling at restaurant stops and horizons
As we drive along scenic oceanside highways, windows down, music
blaring, while he pops in earbuds to drown out
sounds of my carefully curated playlist

Amid sandy beaches and Monet sunsets, he gazes unimpressed much
like I did at all those garish jumpsuits long ago
It was like staring into a mirror of my past—a dirty, cracked, fun
house mirror in which
I had been the apathetic teen sneering at Elvis's tacky kingdom while
my father tried to infuse me with the spirit of rock n' roll,
but I couldn't see past all the rhinestones and velvet ropes

I was too young and stubborn to understand the poetry of it all,
and suddenly, it hit me like a pink Cadillac: this is, in fact,
my karma for Graceland

Now, here I am, miles from Memphis,
but these wind-swept sands of Cape Cod feel as lonely
as the gaudy corridors of Graceland
my son, unfazed, suited with the same look of disdain I once wore
realizing our love for things doesn't transcend generations
sometimes until years later
when we're finally hit with a karmic sucker punch,
delivered by the universe itself,
as the cycle spins, relentless and true, from tacky white mansions
to Cape Cod's deep blue

If We Make it Through the Night

– So much is lost, so many left adrift

In Time

The world was ending
we heard thunderclaps of explosions far off in the distance
warning us over and over
stay indoors

You stood at the window
an open frame to wherever we must go
we danced without music slowly in circles
becoming our own rhythm, our own universe
all those nights ago

Capture the Lightning

beneath a still, soundless, morganite sky
celestial pyrotechnics dance
eyes ignited, copper-hued conductors
sharp and metallic, spark
chasing electric tempests with fervent abandon

rust-tinged bitter heartache
torments the mind
stings like the ripe juice of a lemon on fresh lacerations
salty-red wounded hearts pulse with the suffering of loss
as we brave storms raging

somewhere in the distance, thunder peals the air
filling atmospheres with crackling symphonies

in our darkest sorrow
we measure infinite moments
as we seek to capture the radiance of heaven
set ablaze with sparkling fire

January 10th

A metallic bird falling from the sky
muffled thunder crashes through
ethereal atmospheres

My fragile eggshell mind shatters
as marigold memories pour themselves out
running down, away from me
I cannot save them, or you

You are the black box of my soul
I can no longer recover
locked away behind wrought iron gates
forged of suffering
submerged in heartache

I have lost you
I am
lost

Forgotten the Surface

I would exhale every last breath
to fill your lungs as mine grow still
if only to resurrect you

I would steal a kiss in your final moments
to taste last words never spoken from your lips
as you rise up
I sink lower into depths of knowledge
I've already forgotten the surface

I'm sinking within bitter grief
fast asleep, quilted in roses
pulling me deeper – I know I'm drowning
but I've already forgotten the surface

Waters of disillusion leave deposits on my soul
the everbearing torment of memory and regret
for lost youth, timeworn ambitions, and unrealized dreams
buried within infinities of you and this ocean of longing
one a shroud, the other a tomb
I've already forgotten the surface

Treading water, dancing among dark disorder
I still believe in phrases we breathed
as arms outstretched toward crystalline, radiant skies
grow tired from excavating the depths for something to give,
someone to save,
but I couldn't, and I didn't
I've already forgotten the surface

Anchored

Trembling waves fracture the sunset
casting refractory beams that shimmer and fade
into the rippling sea below
a gilded chalice slips quietly into the deep,
spilling its innocent hues over worn, weathered planks beneath my feet

I search for the other half of my soul in the chaos of crashing tides,
my gaze drifting beyond the blurred horizon, where sky meets sea
salt stings my eyes, mingling with tears

This solitude clings to me like a damp, heavy sweater,
its weight pressing down with every step
cold threads its way through my spine,
a chill with no destination

The vast sky, full of unspoken longings,
calls me to shed the anguish that fills this space
I cast each sorrow into the abyss from which it came,
in this saltwater sanctuary,
I let them go,
anchored by the beauty that remains,
and to which I will one day return

Sometime in the Mourning

I cannot help but stop and look at the numbness of mourning
down into the depths, I plummet into darkness
unforgivingly I go – dull, silent, petrified

Bereavement is a timeless sorrow
its cold fingers wrap around my heart,
like a relentless veil that never lifts,
binding me to memories both sweet and bitter

In silent hours it whispers tales of loss,
and I listen, captive, with tear-stained eyes
to echoes of laughter now turned to sighs

How familiar this prison of genuine grief has become
its icy chains make me shiver
as I clang my overflowing cup of white-hot disconsolation
against steely cold bars, unending

Never quite escaping,
I grasp at fleeting rays of light
drifting on a breeze like sparrow wings
that gently touch my cheeks,
stained with the cherry hue of regret

Broken

Through broken TV screens, I watch everyone go about their lives
celebrating, living, loving
like a film replayed a thousand times
but now seen through the lens of a slivered heart
each fragment a knife, piercing deep, opening wounds, splintering bone

If you have not wandered through the valley
of your own metaphorical death
you cannot fathom this agony
you cannot know my pain
you cannot know me

Labels of shame
from those who left us
wound deep, like a loaded gun
injuring the soul with empty words
a spiritual casualty,
you piece yourself together
knowing there's no surviving
another blow like this
yet with fierce defiance
you dare to love again,
risking it all once more

Society is unkind to women with starving souls
we're told to let go, but not too much,
to move on, but not too quickly
there is no solace in our struggle,
for the world would rather see us doused in darkness and
devoured by the flames of those who claim to "love" us

I wake from nightmares where he survives,
only to tell him we can no longer be
this is my life now, as the sorrow in his eyes
tears my heart from its place
these are the visions that haunt me, even behind closed eyes,
there is no reprieve
I offer them freely – take them from me please

There isn't a cure for complicated grief
but they'll dish out prescriptions like candy—
these rancid type of sweets
with side effects as your dismissed and fed
like a cog into the machine

Spare me your platitudes, please, they are an affront at best
not all of us can subscribe to your fairytale endings
I would go anywhere for a breath of relief,
MAKE. IT. STOP. PLEASE.
but the pain is deaf, indifferent to pleas

I no longer belong anywhere
but this cemetery hillside,
burying pieces of myself, before it's time

Rest does not come in the aftermath
there is no peace for a grief-broken soul
now half-human, half-ghost,
merely a flicker of moments from a past life
that I miss most

I Am Not

I am not the one everyone misses
when days grow long and your absence
carves wounds into cumbersome hearts

I am not the talented hero
the unimaginable creations you wielded
with perfection are now dormant as all things crack, break, and crumble
all around to dust

I am not the family
the ties that bind us
it turns out blood is not thicker than
tear-stained blank pages

I am not the friend
you want to talk to
the one you wonder about
the one you check in on

I am not the one . . .
never have been, never was

I am not the writer, the creative, the essential worker
I have invested a lifetime of hiding behind others
out of focus
an imposter convincing enough
that you do not question it

I am not the one you want or need
I am not who I want or need
I am not missed
but forever missing

Eve After The Fall

Concrete pathways beneath bare feet
lead me again to where you are
concealed within the enigmatic garden

Lush foliage bears perpetual witness
to consequence of mortal sin
my hand reaches to meet your tangled frame's luster
where sunlight still lingers

Empty palms pressed
against naked silhouette
perched upon timeless marble
now liberated

First bites clarify sight
as fresh nectar blushes from your lips
unraveling your distorted, shameful body

I too crave to eat from the Tree of Knowledge
unapologetically and unashamed
revealing it all
until paradise is once again lost

Writing a Poem to a Brick Wall at 4 a.m. on a Thursday

4 a.m., a sacred time for the lost
within stillness of a world at rest
where introspection and darkness collide

Hello there, my silent confidant
of sweet, desolate confinement
oh, how I envy your silence, dear wall
as you bear witness to my soul's depths
offering no judgment, no opinion, no disdain
just sanctuary
for a heart that's lost control

You remember me, how kind
you should, after all
I've been slammed alongside you,
had my back up against you,
been shut out and walled off
and well, in my defense,
I thought you were keeping me out
but maybe
just maybe
you were keeping me in

Everything is a loop
everything is a spiral

Devoid of care, yet somehow you understand
the isolation and sardonic control
together, we navigate this melancholic tint
as I scrape my fingers against your cold surface
I think often why I chose you
and not a mirror

Words tumble from my lips
unfurling like smoke
venomous barbed arrows
shot into the ether
reverberate and collide
where red blood flows warmest
injecting upstream
10ccs of vitriol
this burn
so searing, so familiar

Knowing another restless night awaits
but for now, in the hush of this moment,
talking to a wall at 4 a.m. feels strangely comforting
thank you for this one-sided exchange
from an unmoved audience
for maybe I am just a lost whisper amidst the silence after all

Chasing Echoes

Restless seas tumble
across ancient sand
warm breezes carry in sweet scents of jasmine
as I pull my balcony seat to exotic harmonies calling me home

Warm currents sweep
across uncovered shoulders
lips blossom like ruby chrysanthemums
as I anxiously await your reply
resigned to chasing echoes of a fellow
lost soul

Amazing how cordless lines still tangle
even in opulent paradise
wires cross within digital playscapes

The beauty outside is a fierce temptress
unwavering and steady
as seductive as she may be,
I've become accustomed to wrapping myself in blankets
woven from threads of interdependence

If We Make It Through the Night

If we make it through the night,
will we wake once more to a day kissed with pale lights of dawn,
eyes still shimmering with remnants of our dreams,
staring into smoky-blue hued mornings that promise nothing,
where life stretches out like worn ribbon
frayed at the edges by time's relentless pull?

In that fleeting instant, will we find courage
to embrace ourselves, to hold the ghosts of our past,
to swing open the door to truths we've kept locked away,
and step into the vast, aching emptiness of all we've lost,
who we were and the strangers we've allowed ourselves to become?

If we make it through the night,
if we dare to hope, to believe in the impossible,
do we possess the wild, untamed spirits
to bind our hearts together,
to love with the reckless abandon those who have nothing left to lose,
leaving no one outside the margins?

Anxiety winds through us
haunting the corners of our minds,
can we shatter the fragile cages holding our hearts captive?

Will we find beauty in moments yet to come,
even as time slips away like sand through our fingers,
and so much is lost,
so many left adrift?

If we escape the suffocating night,
into tender arms of a spring that never withers
I pray we'll meet again, as we were before
if we make it,
if we make it through

Swallow

Death has come to dance with me this day,
he takes everything I am in one revolution
without any mercy

We dance without care
we spin and spin,
carving out deepest blood-red wounds
like grooves of worn-out vinyls

I am flung into openness and nothingness
unbuttoning inhibitions,
we swim into dawn's tide pool reflections
that bounce off our backs' chastened armor

It is much easier to deflect this love than accept it
it awakens revelations –
what if they're right?

I open my mouth to speak a truth
as you seal it with a kiss
we both swallow without regret

Beyond the Green Grass

July is the cruelest month
breeding heat waves out of scorched soil
I yearn for nothing more than a soft-landing place
to rest this weary head
something good to hold me, if only for one second longer

I've smelled wilting flowers in the funeral parlor
they smell just like the ones in my backyard
and that green grass
is always greener someplace far from home
the tragedy's always the same, all love is an illusion
within fractured-mirror reflections
of a tattered sundress worn like a shield of memories
behind mascara-smudged eyes,
this girl with a shattered smile knows
there is no cure for the human condition

I did not go gentle into that horrid night
but raged and forged masks in the face of melancholy,
hiding behind them
scribbling words anyplace that would take them,
painting grief in bold indelible brush-stroked stories
sleeping between manuscripts of Fitzgerald, Eliot & Thomas
only to witness
that green light is always just out of reach because
we are nothing but lost time and tragedies of a past life,
unreclaimable

All the love poems have gone sideways
now crumpled up, stuffed inside linen-lined pockets
never to see the light of day, for they may have failed
but the apathy has always got me
when empty-room reminders harbor whispers
of those who never stayed

Alive

– You sang my soul back together
in the heat of darkness
I felt so alive

Tourist

The scent of your leather jacket loiters
inside the corridor within
fleeting moments of an archway embrace

I'm overwhelmed by the urge
to shed my clothing and
subtly slip into it
like a bouquet of roses
with an exaggerated pout
and arched eyebrows

The textural warmth,
an amplified memory of your skin,
brushes my collarbone like your lips once did
hours of inhibitions lost and not giving a single damn

A tourist hidden within
reading lines of poetry
stitched inside, like liner notes of our favorite albums

I weep openly as
our dark hearts connect the dots
shades of black liquidity fill fragile spaces
as I bite your bottom lip

I want to feel something, anything, nothing
you feel safe,
like going home

Downpour

Midnight air is thick with the memory of your breath
warmly brushing my ear

It feels a waste—
sitting here, fingers tracing ghostly curves in the dark

Your taste still fresh upon my lips
like final bites of ripe strawberry
a sweetness bursting on my tongue,
the heat of your skin melts like nectar inside my mouth

Dissolved only by a thunder of surrender,
unraveled, piece by piece,
hanging in air
the pulse of your lips against mine,
a promise never fully savored

a beautiful, aching waste—

All I want is to drown in you—
consumed by the flood of your touch
spilling over,
tracing rivers raging down skin,
until every drop soaks through
filling the spaces you left behind

until nothing else exists but the storm of you,
until I am lost in the downpour

Patient

making out
further down the beach, we drifted
moonlight cast silver whispers on waves

I hadn't spoken a word
for what felt like an eternity

I'll say this: except for the first few minutes,
he didn't act scared
and now he sat,
a silhouette against the horizon

happy at the prospect
that carried us
to the light

September's Breath of Poetry

Darkest night of September
gentle breeze slips through the open window
dancing across the tender curve where the nape
of my neck meets shoulder

Crickets serenade a symphony, gifted by nature
as my lips lift into a radiant smile
foreign emotions flood my form
like a cherished friend's long-awaited return
I do not want this visit to end

Picturing you under star-drenched sky, conceiving thoughts of me
my heart pounding vehemently, like striking typewriter keys
melting ink ebony thick onto paper
hungry for your poetry to fill every part of me

The Lion and the Moon

Emotions rise and fall
I am the sun
born of hellfire
in like a lion
blinding, blood-orange blossoms bursting with enthusiasm

Tides change with swift precision
led by phases
you are the moon, pragmatic and still
darkness surrounds you but does not consume
your effervescent soft glow
a neon sign humming

Constant white noise silences my demons
hugs the curves of my body
envelops me with circumspections only prophets could ascertain
like an ancient magic sprung from the cosmos' vast nothingness
you hold me close to the vest, a Tarot of the Fool
burning with direction toward new beginnings and what is yet to come

Together we are an act of mutually complementing
interaction of opposites
which forces us to move undeniably close to one another
until at last
we are one

Alive

I think I knew I loved you so early on
as we perused pages
at the used book sale on our first date
me with arms encumbered
you were more cautious in choosing

I thought I had ruined it all when
I joked about your taste in music
most 30-year-olds I know don't listen
to Chet Baker and Charlie Parker
an old soul-millennial
I was older than you
but not enough to know better

Secret pains plucked heartstrings
like moody renditions of the jazz
you loved so well
when I shared my not-so-shining moments,
you looked back at me unjudging
with the kindest eyes I had ever seen

I kissed poetry from your lips
as you made me believe in second chances
your warm hand cradled my smile
as I reached up to meet it gently with mine

Alone in the darkness
we whispered set lists of special requests,
you sang my soul back together
in the heat of darkness
I felt so alive

Mixtape

I want to make you a mixtape kind of love
the kind where my hand finds yours
and we don't say much
because we don't need to
where words unspoken slip off the tongue at random,
reckless and unguarded

The kind that makes you wonder
if the end of everything will come with a sunrise or a sunset
desires draped in velvet irony,
the kind that dances with death in the rain
where you find fragments of me,
lingering like ghosts in the machine

I want to be the fall you never saw coming
the kind that's desperate and deep and doesn't let go
to share with you both poetry and storms
to walk beside you in endless adventure
as rain writes our story in liquid shadows on pavement

The kind that, when I'm just a whisper of your past,
I'll still always be stirring in the air like your favorite song
playing in the back of your mind
recollected with a smile
as you repress how my lips once tasted of honey

Anthem

Give me a year of your life, and I shall parcel you one of mine
may it seep through you
blood orange and pomegranate distillations
a vibrancy which seeps into your marrow,
binding with the very fabric of your being
unable to forget the ache
even as it is fading

I have felt the heaviness of too many sorrows,
grief is a weight that crushes
you are a hymn, a quiet prayer whispered in the dark
a rattle, a hum, an anthem
that lingers throughout
a stained-glass reflection casting color that spills across the carpet
climbing walls, painting my pale skin bright
to know you is to glimpse the divine, and in that
I am devout

I remember every flicker of light that has ever danced beside your form
for you are you, and I am only truly myself when I become
the dream of another,
a vision adorned with charms of my own making

And maybe you love obscure things
may you see – that I have loved you
as all dark things love
in the sacred space where shadow and soul coalesce

Startled Air

Five years before
they came to a place
along the sidewalk
where moonlight washed over cracked pavement,
pale as a whispered secret

Turning toward one another, they paused,
eyes flickering with an excitement neither fully understood
he lingered, just a breath away, before finally closing
the space between them
his lips brushed hers, and for a fleeting second,
she was somewhere else —
adrift on a melody she couldn't quite recall —
phrases littered with half-remembered dreams

As their lips parted, the air between them trembling,
trying to capture the unspoken
but no words came,
only the subtle ache of things left unsaid,
floating away on startled air
lost to the night forever

Labyrinths

I plucked a truth from you
not ready to be touched
and the fear it generates is palpable
a void of all-encompassing
vulnerability
as you touch the same
quiet frequencies
pain lives
and plots intricate
escape routes as
your lips create labyrinths
that I get lost
deeper
and deeper
within

Bibliophile

Hidden between waxed wood and leather-bound tomes
a disarming smile gives way to withering put-downs
deepest inner struggles buried well hidden beneath volumes of
barbed observations and the dry rustle of vellum

Trembling dust-laden fingerprints stroke her spine
the one you come back for time and time again
fitted in a gilded dust jacket of gold-rippled rum and rivulets
sinister secrets cleverly cloaked in luscious alabaster clouds

Narcotic tendencies smothered gently
by the heart of everyone who encounters you
forced to face past failures and secrets harbored
lasciviously within the wood-paneled seclusion of this night's rendezvous
inside transcendental blue hour midnights
and the velour caress of
steamy lemon-washed windows
of the shop around the corner

Hard-learned lessons
a honey-eyed loner by heart,
cedar pencil shavings add further intrigue
of this sapiophilic seduction
as we finally reach
the base of it all
dog-eared dalliances of disasters
personify sanguine elegance, and I am
lost in the pull of your pages
you're simply impossible
to ever put down

Seamless

words spilt from your half-open mouth like honey
as the velvety touch of your lips
knitted gently with mine

edible sugar-glazed virtues loitered
as you unpacked both
the sweet and the bitter
seamlessly

in the aftermath of your kiss
the sweet taste of your tongue lingers

Respire

the warmth of your skin mingles
within mists of affection
alternating the rate
molecules evaporate and disperse,
changing your dwindling fragrance

a concentration of excess guilty pleasures
without restraint or moderation
swaying those who haven't already swooned

I would settle
for an existence
if only as a reflection
within your tear-stained eyes

instead, I lie here
exquisitely self-aware,
conscious of your alluring exhales
breathing warm and nervous
on somebody else's neck tonight

Maps

Projections of our moving hands paint frescos upon your ceiling's canvas
I was invited into this moment, well-dressed and looking hungry,
with a strong backbone and sense of empowerment
as hopeful innocence lingered
in this night's black delirium

Shapes shift and dissolve beneath the fog
of your presence above me
your eye's affirming smile
hold the colors of your joy
discovering uncharted territories
listening for a momentary hush,
you vary your rhythm obligingly

Your penmanship, a long-lost love letter
I keep reading, continuously searching for truth and meaning
as my fingers trace along your terrain
memorizing plunging curves like a maritime map
retracing every inch of our
past lives in present tense,
our mortal breaths fleeing easily

I carve my initials upon your heart with generous lips
until all that's left is your name inside my throat
a handful of letters hanging on
until they drift away, unaltered,
unknown

Smolder

distant drifts carry smoke-laden currents
riding night winds
you exhale fumes of deep sighs
lifting high and draping around us like
sanctified frankincense
of by-gone confessions

my ashen fingertips swarm your skin
as our insides smolder with stolen kisses
smoky tendrils of bonfire gripping our hair
as your cold lips burn like the sting of a leather whip
tracing wounds as if they were art
you are captivated by the ache

midnight curtains draw open
to morning's first daybreak
streams of light settle onto stubbed cigarettes
traces of wild revelry punctuated by last night's smudged eyeliner
are offered to fickle gods
and lewd demons tamed by daylight's onslaught

embers glow outside
leaving our torn consciences to douse
the remains of something
that always
kept us
so warm

Bliss

I clutch these beads of sweat around my neck,
intricately tracing the base of my throat
as they break and connect with the liquefaction of clothing
pooled on the floor
rosy complexions flush and fade, turning skin fair
our shared breaths fill the room with lightness and little sighs
each one sweet and new on your mouth
teasing thirsty souls in figured darkness
such bliss melts gently,
as embers die out
quickly and fade
your sweetness loiters, a silken thread of honeyed notes on my tongue,
haunting my thoughts like a memory of love lost to time

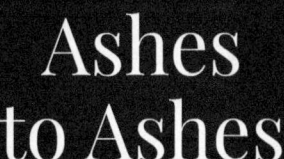

Ashes to Ashes

*— There is a profound beauty within self-destruction
a moth drawn to a flame
dancing towards demise*

Between Insomnia and Fading Lights

Somewhere between insomnia
and dying lights of the periphery
I remember your taillights
flashing red hot against
summer evening
and that parking lot,
your hand on my knee,
how good you smell,
a flicker of streetlight,
haunted empty streets

Everything could dissolve into a noiseless tumble
but we're lost in the heat of each other,
unconscious of the tender hush that surrounds us

The sun's long gone down
but the sear of your lips melts my skin
tonight, your breath whispers on my shoulder
gentle and steady

I wonder why you haven't folded
this hand you're holding
unaware of your strategy
it seems you've played your cards right

Maybe we're murderous
because we're killing time
nevertheless, if all we can do
is fill the glass on your nightstand
half full or half empty
Isn't that worth something?

If I could change anything, I'd leave it be
because we all deserve nice stories

If you're one of the lucky ones
you'll find love somewhere between
the middle and ending
and if you're even luckier
you'll finally wake up
and feel it too

Fade

streetlamps hum into the darkness
illuminating all the glittering-gold lies
as the warm spring evening approaches with first wild promises

my heart navigates toward
this unexpected kaleidoscope of emotions
that spill out to form life's new normal

the lights grow more lustrous
as the earth falters from the sun,
pursuing you in eternal graceless circles
against delphinium-blue skies

all the years lost struggle upon my lips
as our first opal kiss dissolves
until we form the same breath

long-held perceptions of endearment
cascade quickly and fade
back into warm obscurity
like an uninvited guest

The Movie's Ending

I always felt this way about him

I am not sure he knew this then, however,
this fondness and trust was rare
and I appreciated equally the similarities and differences we shared

On an overcast spring day, when he accepted
my offer to see a movie,
it felt like the sun shined on me from a whole other direction

I grabbed onto him like kite strings floating above the horizon
and permitted myself to live in this moment,
no matter how fleeting I knew it was

Loss brings with it an appreciation of "little things"
like crumpled-up receipts lining cupholders,
a refreshing reminder of the human condition

Feeling like I no longer had the energy to survive another moment,
I hummed along to The Smiths lyrics playing on repeat in my head,
"driving in your car, I never never want to go home"
and I truly didn't

Shared laughs became life preservers

Navigating the labyrinthian maze of downtown parking
we finally found a spot
It was such a novelty to be concerned
with something as trivial as missing opening previews

The rain began to pour, and he told me we'd meet up inside
I began to run toward the shelter of the glowing marquee,
then stopped and turned to watch him fumble his keys
and get soaked while he fed money into the meter
I didn't want to leave him, half out of guilt he was getting soaked
and half because it felt so good just to be in his proximity

Steam rose as rain hit warm pavement,
I thought about how cold the rain felt and how, in a
few minutes we would be inside the air-conditioned theater,
how uncomfortable that would feel,
but strangely,
nothing felt weird or uncomfortable within that moment

I had never seen anyone savor popcorn with such devotion
his love for it was almost reverent
silly as it sounds, popcorn always carries a piece of him for me now

As the movie began, a strong feeling of melancholy
washed over me; I knew this too eventually had to end
my mind reminded me insistently
I couldn't bear to watch another ending

Veiled dimness disguised the crying
my tears flowed freely as I hoped
they wouldn't catch the light from the projector's reflection
and be noticed

There was so much to lose,
confusing themes of friendship and love indescribably
glossed over the ephemeral fading matinee
having someone close whom I thought so much of felt safe
my heart was obliterated, but I could still feel it beating

I wanted to reach out and hold his hand
because I was scared of so many things, but I knew
it would come across all wrong
each frame's beautiful symmetry slipped away
the end credits would soon be rolling, and our time together
was running out

I knew this gnawing anxiety, the dread of another loss, another ending
It was easier to ignore the truth and linger, preserved in this
contentment,
for just one more fleeting moment longer

Oh, So Tired

I'm Jack's typewriter,
growing darker day by day
frost white, to light tan,
grey-blue, to dark grey

I thought I was still young
but these bloodless veins
show indifference and
as numb as I've become
it's easy to get tangled up
in phthalo-green haze of incense
no closer to the exit
or walking away

I never claimed to be a poet
but I've read and re-read enough verse and prose
long enough to know
I've been left for dust
on the side of the road less traveled
and I'm oh so tired
but I'll kindly take
your sympathetic smile any day
and hope one day, it all mattered

Last calls have been shouted
and the bars are all closing
so, let's trip the light fantastic
seeing sanity within sadness
because none of us is ever
getting out of this life alive

The Sweet and the Stung

Wire-pulled automatons
our silhouetted frameworks
slid through slowly
revealing the bruises of our souls

Radium-tainted smiles
illuminated serpentine paths of our choosing
for "the truth is rarely pure and never simple"
we breathed in Wilde and subconscious
as a delicate, three-letter thread unraveled
gossamer unspoken desires

Vacant-faced one-sided ghosts
between midnight nothings,
we watched love play out on reels before us
in between the eclipse of kiss-or-kill flavored celluloid
my wordy wounds flushed your technicolor cheeks
underneath a grayscale moon

Archiving past inadequacies of fate and future
I dipped my finger into life's hive
and from the void,
pulled out
both
the sweet
and the stung

Under the Overpass

The trees are budding in February
seeing something as confused as I am in nature,
makes me feel less alone

We've been wild, like the weather
as rapture drips from our lips
and lingers
we run from soft nightmares

Let's meet under the overpass
where our silhouettes blend within
water's glossy reflection
so you can feel the pulse of
poetry stuck inside me,
right under my lowest left rib
where ache and art intertwine

Go ahead, try to pluck it out
I've tried my damnedest, knuckles raw
from this vault of rust and echoes
confined like Houdini, who too grappled
with that fine line between life and vanishing

For trust is a wealth I've never had the pleasure of accruing
but somehow, you carry all the pastel money
and always let me pass go
no matter what the weather

East Coast Heartbreak

We were too afraid to love anyone
but have all the time in the world; we lie
too scared to live
we waste time building cages
and penning our obituaries
just the way we want them to read

Already dripping wet with these wounds I run from
more spring tears will soon be shed upon us
dissolved first only
by the heat of summer pavement
or the fire of our skin

Grey Area

I gave my soul blindly
casting it into the unknown
like a poet freeing words to the night,
craving soft replies in return

You would think, in a world
so tangled with dreams and desires
you would search for me,
following the thread of what could have been
but you drifted away,
lost in the shimmer of things unseen

You never knew
how like a tree, you took root in me
your presence seeping quietly
into the corners of my heart,
spreading through to
where day and night blur into something
indistinguishable, something tender

In the velvet hush of evening
nothing stands clear –
the line between black and white dissolves
and all that remains is delicate grey,
a place where truth and illusion
mingle like old lovers

Hold me now, as the world softens
let us linger in this moment,
where everything feels suspended,
caught between the past and what might come
here, in quiet convergence
we are neither lost nor found
but simply together
bound by the quiet ache of something
deep and unspoken,
something that belongs only to us

Time Bomb Girl

I'll take your warm body in any room,
instead, I keep walking into vacant ones
surrounded by the faceless crowds of a world that never knew you
so much of me has slipped away along this elusive journey

Suppose I did smile fantastically for a moment
I have made it this far, stubborn and disastrous
no longer immune to crescendos of rapture

Question this bravery
call it by its rightful name,
at its best, impossible
let us name it for what it truly is,
not marvelous, but impossible to bear

Even the great Socrates was ruined by Athens
the magnitude of beauty does not afford us peace
just shades of a time-bomb girl

Lighting the wick of the mind's catastrophe
you diffuse through, undeterred, unbroken
imploding together, we shatter the sky

Ashes to Ashes

If life's about the getting and keeping
I've given up much to moments fleeting

If life's about things to have and to hold
I've measured sunsets ablaze red and gold

The cost, comfort, friendship, and most of all pleasure –
I've danced wild and wicked amongst these endeavors

In life, it looks that I lose for asking
such little pay it seems for the tasking

For all the hurting, heartbreak, and distress
I'll gladly exchange some and take up much less

Leave the sharp stones alongside the highway
avoid all those in grass-covered byways

The weariness of it all, sins of passions, and deeds of war
to questions unanswered
what was it all for?

Cipher

What purpose do I find within wistful loveliness?
to resist easy torment, the false purity of mountains
where everyone forgets how Icarus once flew
not failing but fading in triumph
a simple plight against the sun's brutality
or perhaps just the arrangement of inconvenient light

I've tasted deep pain meant only for stronger palates
and for a fleeting moment, savored deep happiness alongside
a lonely, tragic monologue
behind ochre lens' timeless story
far beneath serrated surface tension lie depths beyond measure

You led me to the River Styx,
Latin for hate
I hate myself, and you hate me too
now I've swallowed the coin under my tongue,
seeking release from corrosions against my weary palate

Souls entwined in hate
for no fire or freshness can challenge the ghosts
we carry on countless days
dead seasons fill life's climbing grave
In twisted existence,
I am but a cipher to save
a mangled body drowning in fountain-heart puddles
running from ourselves only brings us nearer to reflections of suffering
let me drown
so I may be reborn
so I may live

Gilded Oblivion

In neon-lit alleys of the mind
she dances within the contours, a desperate waltz
of fear and isolation

Feeling the sting, embracing the need
within chaos
seeking answers and truth
inside the savage beauty of
our shattered youths

This one's gonna hurt the worst,
rip the bandage, let it burst
raw crimson truth spilling
eyes wide like saucers
this affliction,
a most relentless form of wicked,
blood-letting, gnawing insides

From soaring highs to crushing lows
she drowns sorrows
and escapes hurting through
bruised-hued dawn of new morning's heartache
chasing gilded oblivion

The moon weeps in her darkness
a silent witness under stardust's veil,
for the night will hold her close
but never truly let her in

The Taste of Arsenic

The taste of arsenic lingers on my lower lip
a stripe of Scheele's green pigment bites at my mouth
it moves slowly through my system
toxic as it is intoxicating

Art begets life, and all life is suffering
this mirage is only
a fickle trick of light

There's mercury in the vermillion
poisoning the wallpaper,
dying the clothing,
blushing my cheek,
corrupting your kiss,
tainting goodbyes

There is a profound beauty within self-destruction
a moth drawn to a flame
dancing towards demise
this is Armageddon you tell me
and we're all gonna burn in the end

I'd take the inferno
it's much faster
than this slow-drip sear of pain
but when you live with the taste of it long enough
you learn to like the flavor

The Fading Asters

I cup my hand to my ear
and pretend I can hear the ocean
but all I hear is the echo of us

Sitting comfortably on your old sofa
as scenes of our love
flicker and fade like old reels of film

Your smile – oh how it reached
up embracing your eyes
the finest lines sealed our fates
my soul chases the warmth of its light in the afterglow

Ashes in our hearts parted ways
with promises they once held
as the sky darkened
sparklers plumed
against the ink of night
we slow danced
and you sang in my ear
I could listen to your voice forever
the way it cradles my heart

Riding in your car
we sang with reckless abandon
our voices ricocheting off mountainsides
chasing the tender blush of dawn's first light

Inside the mirror of your heart
I saw the reflection of my own
and within the sanctuary of your arms
I discovered my truest home

A place where time stood still
and I want it all back
before the purple asters die
I'll take them inside
hang them to dry
press them between pages
of a book where we were never on the same page
and make peace with what remains

Afterthought

I went to walk down by the river,
where the current hummed like
a far-off conversation,
half-heard, always out of reach,
beating soft against the banks,
carrying cigarette butts, broken bottles,
and drifting dreams of people I'll never meet

The moon was a ghost tonight,
sliding between shadows,
and I thought of you—
how everything just moves on,
whether we want it to or not

You speak as if I'm already gone,
floating between syllables,
a fading thought that never quite landed
I was never meant to stay—
like catching the last train
and forgetting where you were supposed to be headed
a wanderer with no map,
slipping through the fog of a dream
you woke from too late

Yes, we danced, if you can call it that,
not to music but to the rhythm of tires on wet pavement,
late-night highways stretching forever,
and the sound of waves lapping at some unseen shore—
places we never went,
lovers we never quite became

Your smile still tastes like yesterday,
but I've forgotten how to hold it,
how to place it gently in a corner of my mind
without it turning into dust

Funny how I was always just a flash,
a match strike in the dark,
meant to burn out before you even noticed

Now, I see you like a stranger on the corner—
we nod, we share a look,
and then it's gone,
a polite exchange between two people
who'll never know the end of each other's stories
It's always the things we don't say
that haunt us—
the words that hang between the lines,
drifting like cigarette smoke in a room
we'll never return to

And so, I remain,
not quite a memory,
just something that fades as the night grows deeper,
an afterthought
you never truly had

The Season of Holding On

*— If light could heal what's broken,
the morning could hold me
the way the night once did*

Lost Dreamer

Summer skies weep
yet refuse to wash away
this dull ache
inside my hollow nerves

I want to tell you everything
I feel inside me
but all the words
die upon my lips

As the calendar bleeds into July
leaving behind only
smoke and fading memories
ash and numbness

Our halcyon breath grows faint
what-ifs unfold like dahlias
in meadows of my thoughts
I never want to leave this place

A world spins on immeasurably indifferent
I'm a lone dreamer, a solitary architect of fantasy
etching sonnets into sand,
knowing they will be swept away
by time's dispassionate tides

Nothing ever lasts forever
it haunts my half-closed eyes
inside this window
where silent stars hold nightly vigil

In the end, I'm just a lost dreamer
confused and craving
inside a world
that has forgotten
how to dream

The Marble Faun
After Nathaniel Hawthorne & Edith Bouvier Beale

To the days of grace and grandeur,
a riot of color and chaos
grows unchecked
forgotten arias sung to ghosts of her past
echoes of Hawthorne's spirit whisper through crumbling walls

Viridescent ribbons of fountain grass spill out onto
abandoned footpaths where she dances in the spirit of Little Edie
in a skirt worn thin
connecting the spaces inside her heart
where fertile and wasteland collide

Grey gardens begot of forgotten dreams
where the Marble Faun once held court
where have all the gorgeous days gone?
they hang in air like traces of bittersweet perfume

A freshly pricked finger sheds scarlet trajectories
down rusted railings
spilling upon marigold petals
sunlit wisps vibrant and golden
their citrusy sweetness grounded in earth,
reminiscent of summer's full-bloomed gardens

Beauty fades like last rays of sunlight before dusk
in eccentric fashion and spirited monologues,
she moves through rooms like the specter of her former self
screeching blue jays, the only witnesses to her unraveling
yet now she glides through walls
a presence of myth and art
where history both burdens and balms

Even in the face of ruin
there is a quiet strength
a persistent heartbeat
a refusal to be silenced

The Stray

The sun cast its warm glow through large windows
of the hazy refuge on a quiet city corner,
the aroma of freshly brewed espresso mingles
with the soft hum of conversations
this little haven appears plucked from inside
a Bohemian architect's fever dream

Your voice, dripping like viscous honey, cuts through air
I thought I was merely stopping by, but you know I take my coffee
black, with a hint of sugar
like a dream-swallowing void with a touch of sweet

This summer's been different
we sip in silence and let the bitter brew bandage our wounds
and broken parts we didn't like
both of us a mismatched collection of thrift store discards
connected to feelings of disarray
aren't we all just trying to reinvent the wheel?

Peace was a pasture I never found, but this little corner of the world
is the closest I've come
maybe peace is a myth
forged by fools to comfort the broken-hearted

As afternoon light begins to cast long shadows,
we continue our silent communion
the world outside seems distant,
a blur of noise and pandemonium that
doesn't penetrate our little sanctuary

You lean back, your eyes reflecting a mix of curiosity
and something deeper,
perhaps a shared understanding of unspoken burdens we both carry
fragments of—a series of misadventures that felt like
lifetimes compressed into days
you listen not with pity, but with rare and precious genuine interest

We can talk about anything, but we talk about music,
the kind that speaks to souls and makes you feel less alone
you are forever the keeper of stories, snippets of life
that seem both familiar and foreign
and I realize how truly little we know, yet how much we understand
life has ways of pulling people apart
still, there is hope that maybe, just maybe, we can find contentment
in fleeting moments of connection

I feel a strange sense of calm; all the madness seems a little less daunting
perhaps peace isn't a myth after all, but something we find in the most
unexpected places,
with the most unexpected people
and so, we wander on, forever searching,
but now with a glimmer of hope
that we will all find what we are looking for one day

The Season of Holding On

The wind's now shifted, tugging trees
the last of summer's warmth clings to the air
leaves rust in the quiet morning

Cliffs are wrapped in thin fog
the smell of salt and wood-smoke mingle
as the amber sun rises slow
painting the waves in shades of golds and grays
If light could heal what's broken
morning could hold me
the way night once did

The autumn leaves fall like whispers —
a farewell, an invitation
a promise of the season that asks us
to let go, even as we hold on

But I'll stay a little longer
and linger in fading warmth
before the cold sets in
before the East Coast morning
steals me away
once again

Unapologetic

I've picked up the language of the Underworld
its rhythm of despair
I know the pulse of both worlds
where darkness isn't a cage but a companion,
leading me through nighttime roads

I'm no longer afraid of the dark; I drive into it
old scars turning into canvas
rebirth is not about pretending the past never happened,
it's about climbing over it, shedding it like second skin

Now I walk with eyes wide open,
carrying the weight of a thousand winters in my chest
within my bones hums a quiet power
like a forgotten song
that only I remember

Like Persephone, I am not a victim of fate
I am its author
its keeper
soil turns in my hands
because I will it so
and from cracks in stone
life pushes forth
undaunted
unapologetic
this
you see
is true power
to fall and rise again
to carry darkness
and chase light

pomegranate-seeded tragedy
tethered me here
trapped between worlds

but now I shape the rhythm of my own rebirth
time is elastic
it bends for me
stretching and contracting
like the wings of Icarus approaching the sun

I wander through the quiet, still space
between seconds
rewriting the rules of fate with a loaded typewriter

Spring does not come because it is time
but because I breathe it into being
flowers don't just bloom
they erupt in defiance

No longer a figure of myth,
but living embodiment
of the eternal cycle—
a dramatic flourish of light and dark,
a testament of transcendence and transformation
embracing the raw, untamed truth
of what lies beneath

Acknowledgments

Authoring this book has been a process of both creation and reflection, and I couldn't have done it without the people who stood by me along the way. Every moment of support, whether big or small, has carried me to this point.

To everyone who inspired these words—whether you know it or not—you've left a mark on my heart, and this book is a reflection of that. Thank you for the lessons, the love, and the stories that became poems. Without you, there would simply be no poetry.

To the East Coast and its vast beauty for providing solace, inspiration, and refuge.

And to every reader who wanders through these pages—thank you once again for reading my heart in paper form and seeking the elusive thread of meaning in poetry and the messiness that is the human condition—may you find whatever it is you need here.

–Lastly, to F. Scott & Zelda Fitzgerald, The Smiths, and Julian Casablancas (for personal reasons)

**And Miles who would like me to set the record straight.... He really did enjoy our trip to the Cape (for the most part) and feels everyone should experience those sunsets at least once in their lifetime.

About The Author

Amy Laessle-Morgan is a poet/writer based in Southeast Michigan with a BA in Communication from Oakland University. *East Coast Heartbreak* is her debut poetry collection. Amy sustains her creative expression through the art of words, captured moments in photography, music, art, design, and film. When not writing she enjoys the solace of her garden, reading poetry, collecting records and playing Bass guitar.

Amy's work has been published in the 2020 — 2024 editions of *Sterling Script: A Local Author Collection*, *Unsent Love Letters: An Anthology*, *Poetic Reveries Magazine*, *Poetic Reveries Anthology*, *Artifex Literary Magazine* and *Gypsophila Art And Literary Magazine*. She has also been a contributor to Squirrel Cane Press and a featured collaborative artist for the 2021 New York City concert series *Sounds Rising from Words*.

Her poetry can also be found on Instagram where she writes as @ultramarine_poetry.

www.ingramcontent.com/pod-product-compliance
Lightning Source LLC
Chambersburg PA
CBHW051657040426
42446CB00009B/1175